THE GREATEST
DIY Tips
IN THE WORLD ®

by

Chris Jones and Brian Lee

Illustrated by Graham Robson

Public Eye Publications

A Public Eye Publications Book

www.thegreatestintheworld.com

Illustrations:
Graham Robson, 'Drawing the Line'
info@dtline.co.uk

Cover design:
Setsquare Creative Design Consultants

Cover photo:
Clive Nichols
www.clivenichols.com

Layout design:
Bloomfield Ltd.

Copy editor:
Bronwyn Robertson
www.theartsva.com

Series creator / editor:
Steve Brookes

This first edition published in 2005 by
Public Eye Publications, PO Box 3182,
Stratford-upon-Avon, Warwickshire CV37 7XW

Text and Illustrations Copyright © 2005 - Public Eye Publications

'The Greatest In The World' Copyright © 2004 - Anne Brookes

A CIP catalogue record for this book is available from the British Library
ISBN 1-905151-03-9

Printed and bound by Ashford Colour Press Limited, Gosport, Hampshire PO13 0FW

I would like to dedicate this book to my wonderful Mum and Dad, Thelma and Bill - they taught me well!

Also a special dedication to my ever-loving wife Cathy for years of encouragement and patience, and my two wonderful sons Peter & Mark.

Chris

With loving thanks to my daughter, Dawn, whose time and effort putting everything together on the PC neatly hid my lack of computer literacy!

A particular dedication, also, to my friend and work colleague Guy Burtenshaw, without whose encouragement to join him and the team at shows around the UK, my part in this book would never had happened.

Brig

Contents

Foreword...

Many of us like to dabble at DIY from time to time and, if we are honest, with varying degrees of success. When I decided to add a DIY tips book to our expanding library of publications, I had no doubt in my mind who should write it!

It was during the late 90's, when I was touring the UK, presenting gardening shows on stage for a major DIY and garden store that I first met Chris and Brian. They were presenting DIY demonstrations to audiences who would sit totally engrossed, being informed and entertained as Chris and Brian imparted their years of knowledge and expertise with flair and humour. Within a half-hour show they would have dispensed numerous tips and ideas and audience members would linger to dig for a little more advice and engage in conversation with these two likeable chaps. No-one ever walked away without a smile on their face!

What you see with Chris and Brian is exactly what you get - two sincere, genial tradesmen who really know their stuff. Both have had a lifetime of experience in all areas of DIY with Chris specialising in plumbing and electrics whilst Brian was up to his neck in paint and wallpaper. Between them they have also covered carpentry and general building. When I asked them to collaborate on a DIY tips book they fell about laughing – then, thankfully, they agreed!

The result is what you have before you now – a great little DIY tips book! It may not contain an answer to every DIY question you have but I can guarantee that you will pick it up and refer to it again and again. Maybe you want to work out how many rolls of wallpaper you need for the spare bedroom; how to easily filter lumpy paint or how to unblock a sink. It's all here. Now you can begin to enjoy your DIY.

Good luck!

Steve Brookes
Series Creator / Editor

The Greatest DIY Tips In The World

Quality counts

It is always worth buying the best paintbrushes that you can afford as, with a bit of care, they can be used many times without the annoyance of the bristles falling out mid stroke. If possible, choose paintbrushes that have bristles with split ends as this means a quality brush! To add a little interest to your brush choosing it is worth noting that the bristles on 'pure bristle' brushes are taken from wild pigs or boars residing in China and India. The Chinese bristles are invariably black, very strong and premium quality. Indian pig bristles, in contrast, vary in colour, are coarser, longer and not so strong. Cheaper brushes contain a mixture of pig bristle and horsehair. This gives a softer brush.

Choosing wallpaper

Remember the following tips when choosing rolls of wallpaper:

- Rolls of similar wallpaper will always carry a 'batch number'. To complete a whole room, always choose rolls with the same batch number. Similar looking rolls of paper but with different batch numbers could have a slightly different colouring which isn't noticeable in the shop but will stick out like a sore thumb on the wall!

- A large, bold wallpaper pattern will always make a small room look even smaller.

- Light patterns on a light background will give the impression of space in a room.

- A small random pattern will help to camouflage bumpy or uneven walls.

- A striped pattern only looks really good when the surface is perfectly even.

Sticking doors and windows

It is really annoying when a newly painted door or window decides to stick. With doors this can be avoided by rubbing the door edges with a candle after the paint has dried and before you try closing the door. A film of talcum powder around the door edge can have the same effect.

For windows you should allow the paint to dry thoroughly and then spray both painted edges with furniture polish. Rub this gently with a soft cloth before closing the windows.

Stop-cock knowledge

Make sure that all members of your household know the exact positions of the water stop valves in your house and how to turn them off in an emergency. Remember to open and close the valves once a year to make sure that they are working properly, and lubricate the taps if necessary with a few drops of oil to ensure that everyone can close them easily when required.

Storing brushes and rollers

Once you have finished washing your paintbrushes, give them a final rinse in fabric conditioner to keep them really soft. As soon as your paint brushes are completely dry spend some time running an old comb through the bristles to smooth them out and remove any loose ones. Brushes are then best stored hanging down but only if the bristles can be supported and not allowed to rest on a surface otherwise they become permanently bent and misshapen. If you cannot achieve this, then wrap the bristles in tissue paper and hold them together with an elastic band. Paint rollers should be allowed to dry naturally, removed from their housings and handles, and stored on end.

Window masking

If you use strips of masking tape to protect window glass when painting the frames then be sure to remove it from the glass as soon as possible. If you leave it until the paint has completely dried you risk the chance of pulling off some of the new paint which will have dried across the edge of the tape. You may also get an adhesive residue left on the glass if you leave the tape there for too long.

Decorating conditions

Natural daylight and good ventilation are the ideal conditions for decorating. If you have central heating then turn it off as the heat from radiators can cause uneven drying of paint and wallpaper paste. Circulating air through a room is the best for drying any decorated surface.

Stronger sandpaper

Sand and emery paper can be made stronger and thus will last longer if you criss-cross the back of the sheets with masking tape.

Mixing wallpaper paste

When mixing wallpaper paste always make a stiff mix. Add the paste powder to cold water rather than water to the powder and stir with a piece of wood. This will avoid getting a lumpy mix. Leave for five minutes and put the wooden stick back in the middle of the bucket. If the stick stands up, then the mix is the correct consistency and is ready to use.

Non slip drilling

When drilling into potentially slippery surfaces such as metal or ceramic tiles, first stick a piece of masking tape onto the surface over the spot where you want to drill. This should prevent the drill bit from slipping. For tiles use a glass drill bit instead of a masonry bit. If the hole you need to drill is over 6mm in diameter then drill a pilot hole with a smaller drill bit. Never use the hammer action on a drill, you may crack the tile.

Steel wool gives a fine finish

To give a really perfect fine surface to decorative wood try using fine steel wool as the final 'sanding' before varnishing. Go about the job gently and work along the grain of the wood. If you go across the grain you will invariably make scratches on the wood.

Get radiators checked

If you find that you seem to be constantly 'bleeding' radiators to remove trapped air then seek professional advice as something is plainly not right and could lead to a more serious problem if left unchecked.

Bathroom repairs

Always make sure that you put the plug in the sink or bath if you are doing any work on the taps, shower or anything in the bathroom involving small parts. If you don't, there is a good chance that a small part will invariably be lost down the plug hole!

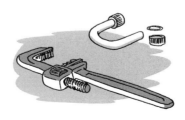

Long painting jobs

If you cannot finish your painting job in one day and intend to continue the next morning, or if you have to stop painting for a short while, then don't bother washing out your brushes or rollers. Instead simply wrap them tightly in plastic kitchen wrap (cling-film) or aluminium kitchen foil to keep the air from drying out the paint and store them in a cool place. The next morning they will be ready to use immediately.

Removing wallpaper

Old wallpaper can be difficult to remove. A solution of equal parts vinegar and warm water, applied to the paper and allowed to soak in will make removal a lot easier. For more stubborn areas try increasing the amount of vinegar in the solution. Before attempting to remove wallpaper borders try loosening the strong adhesive with a hairdryer before using the vinegar and water solution.

Smooth bath sealant

To achieve an even, smooth finish when resealing around a bath, put on a rubber glove and dip your fingers in warm, soapy water. Run a soapy finger along the newly-applied sealant whilst applying even pressure. An equally good way of getting a nice finish is to level the sealant with an ice cube.

Dust-free door painting

A sheet of newspaper or cardboard placed under a door will prevent dust being picked up by the brush when painting. The use of two wooden or plastic door wedges, one each side, will keep the door firmly in position so that both sides can be easily painted.

Fill in stages

If you have large, deep holes or cracks to fill in plaster then
be patient and do the job in two stages. Half fill first and
leave to dry before completing the job. This way you will
ensure even drying of the filler and avoid surface cracking
later on.

Faster filing

A file is one of those tools which, if it's not cared for and stored correctly can become pretty useless. Here are a few tips for keeping your files up to scratch:

Always protect your files from contamination by water or grease which can make them less effective and from getting knocked and chipped. For these reasons it is a good idea to keep your files in your toolbox wrapped in a cloth.

Regularly use a wire brush to keep the grooves of your files clean and work along the grain of the file rather than against it.

Filing aluminium can be tricky as the metal filings soon get stuck in the teeth of the file. To avoid this happening, coat the file in paraffin or rub some blackboard chalk over the teeth of the file before filing. If your file's teeth do become clogged then either roll a small ball of putty or Blu-Tak over the grooves to remove any small particles, or stick a piece of masking tape firmly over the file and rub it down into the grooves. When you peel the tape off any particles that were stuck in the grooves of the file will then be stuck to the tape!

Damp brushes are best

It is always best to dampen a brush before use as this will given a more even application of the paint. When using latex paints the brushes should be dampened with water whereas, for oil-based paints you should use paint thinner. Always use paper towels to remove excess water or thinner before using the brush.

Spotting a leaking pipe

If you are not sure of the location of a small leak in a pipe then cover the suspected area with very soapy water. Bubbles will instantly appear over the hole. This tiny leak can then be temporarily repaired by rubbing the area with petroleum jelly and either tying a cloth around this part of the pipe or wrapping with plumber's tape. Remember that this is not a permanent solution!

Ladder marks

If you need to lean a ladder against a wall or window frame where it could leave visible marks then avoid this problem by slipping an old sock over the ends of the ladder before use.

Warm paint

Paint will be easier to apply with better coverage and less
drips if you stand the tin of paint in a bowl of warm water
for half an hour before use. This is especially useful for
enamel of laquer paints which can thicken considerably
on a cold day.

Paint samples

Always buy a few sample pots of paint before choosing a colour. Paint each sample onto the two sides of a corner of the room to be painted. The way a colour looks will change due to the way the light reflects off the painted surface. Using samples in a corner like this will allow you to see these differences.

Lining paper

Using lining paper is a great way of hiding any small blemishes, particularly on walls that have seen lots of filling work and other repairs. The paper can then be painted or used as a base for wallpapering. If the surface is to be wallpapered then the lining paper should always be hung horizontally to avoid the coinciding of paper joints and to give the best possible bonding strength.

More efficient radiators

Because radiators are positioned next to a wall some of the heat will be adsorbed into the wall itself. You can increase the amount of heat radiated into the room by fixing sheets of thick aluminium foil onto the wall behind the radiators with the shiny surface outward. Heat is effectively reflected back off the foil into the room.

Fishy smell

Never ignore a fishy smell in a room. If no one has recently been cooking seafood then it could indicate an electrical fault which has resulted in the overheating and burning of plastic. Check all electrical appliances that are switched on. If the cause is not obvious then you may want to call in an electrician.

Paint variations

Even though tins of paint are labelled as being the same colour, different batches of paint may vary slightly. To avoid any noticeable differences always buy enough paint to complete the whole job in one go and from the same batch. This should be clearly marked on the tins.

Cleaning shower heads

Mineral deposits from the water can eventually collect inside a shower head rose and block the outlet holes. To clean the rose, remove it and soak overnight in a bowl of vinegar. A needle or piece of fine wire can be used to clear the more stubborn deposits from holes. Before reassembling, rinse the rose well in cold water. Run the shower for a while before use.

Tidy sandpaper

To keep all your wayward pieces of sandpaper and emery cloth in one place use an old clipboard with a thick piece of cardboard placed on top as a cover to prevent the sheets from curling.

Paintbrush support

Tying a piece of string across the open top of a tin of paint will provide support for the wet brush as well as being a useful means to wipe off excess paint from the brush.

Blu-Tak on wallpaper

If the kids have put up posters in their bedrooms using Blu-Tak, removing it can be a problem and may tear the wallpaper. It will, however, come off the paper really easily if you first warm it for a few seconds with a hairdryer.

Slipping screwdriver

Trying to insert a screw into an awkward place can be a tricky job. To make it easier, put a small piece of putty or Blu-Tak onto the screw head first. The screwdriver is then less likely to slip.

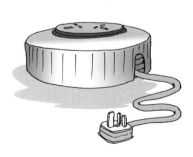

Safe saw

When you buy a wood saw, many will not come with
any protection for the teeth of the saw other than the
cardboard wrapper. Storing a saw without the teeth
covered is bad for the saw and dangerous for you! You
can make a protective sleeve by splitting a length of
rubber garden hose and putting this over the teeth or
cutting a 1" wide strip of tongue and groove flooring,
placing the saw's edge in the groove and securing to the
saw blade with rubber bands.

Paraffin brush cleaner

After using oil-based paints, brushes can be cleaned effectively using paraffin. Place the brushes in a jar of paraffin overnight. The paint from the brushes will fall to the bottom of the jar and the clear paraffin above can be re-used. Finally wash the brushes in warm, soapy water and dry well before storing.

Battery care

Batteries kept in a warm environment will quickly lose their charge so ensure that they are kept in a cool place. Rechargeable batteries should always be recharged immediately after use and should never be stored in a 'flat' state. Even fully charged batteries should be recharged every two months if they are not being used.

Beware cheap tools

This may sound patently obvious but it is worth saying. When it comes to buying tools you really do get what you pay for. Cheap tools may seem like a good bargain but ultimately they will either let you down or give you below par performance. Buy the very best you can, even if you have to wait a while. You will then have tools that you will be more inclined to look after and hence they will last much longer.

Lump-free paint

If you are using a tin of paint that has been used before and stored, it may still have a few lumps in it after stirring well. Avoid even the smallest lumps ruining your painting by taking the trouble to strain the paint through a pair of tights or stockings before use.

Rust-free tools

Tool boxes stored in garages and sheds may at some point get damp inside which could lead to rusting of tools. A few small packets of silica gel (such as those often found in the packaging of electrical goods) or mothballs placed in the tool box will absorb any moisture in the air and prevent rust formation.

Memorable measurements

When doing DIY tasks, avoid the need to find something to write measurements on by sticking a strip of masking tape onto your ruler or measuring tape. When the job is done remove the masking tape and discard, but put on a fresh piece ready for next time.

Paint kettle

Professional decorators usually transfer paint from the shop-bought tin into a smaller and more portable container with a handle called a 'paint kettle'. You will probably find it useful to do the same. It is a good idea to line the paint kettle with aluminium foil as you can throw this away when you have finished. This means that previously used paint doesn't contaminate the newer paint when you come to use the paint kettle again.

Seasoned putty!

Freshly applied window putty is very attractive to birds as they love the taste of the linseed oil it contains. They will think twice about eating it if you mix a little black pepper with the putty before you use it!

Fitting positions

When decorating it is useful to remember the positions of wall fittings so that you can easily find the plugged holes to refit them after the job is finished, instead of poking around with a small screwdriver. This can be easily done by pushing matchsticks into the holes as soon as you remove the fittings. Then you simply push the matchsticks back through newly hung wallpaper as the holes they make will be hidden by the replaced fitting.

Wallpapering finishing touches

When you have finished hanging the wallpaper wipe over any paint work and wallpaper seams with a damp sponge – rinsing the sponge often in warm water. Finally, with a permanent felt tip pen, write on the top of the door frame how many rolls of wallpaper you used in that room - it we help you to remember in years to come!

Rescuing a paintbrush

If a paintbrush becomes rock hard with old paint and all other efforts have failed, there is still a chance that you can rescue it. This is good news, particularly if the paintbrush is a high quality one. First suspend the hard paintbrush for a day with its bristles submerged in raw linseed oil. Then, wearing rubber gloves, rinse the bristles in warmed turpentine solution, working with your fingers to remove all the loosened deposits of old paint. Finally rinse the brush well in warm, soapy water.

Cheap picture hangers

When hanging a lightweight fixture on the wall, instead of searching around for the elusive small picture hook, try stapling, taping or gluing a ring pull from a drink can to the back of the fixing and hanging it from a small nail in the wall.

Cleaning paintwork

To clean paintwork you often need something that will do the job without scratching the paint surface. An old bath loofah, cut into pieces and used with detergent, is ideal for the job. The best liquid to use for cleaning white paint is easily made by boiling a few onions in three pints of water until soft. Drain off the water and use it with soap to clean the paintwork.

Repairing holes in vinyl

Small holes in a vinyl or linoleum floor can be repaired by using a wax crayon. Find a crayon of a similar colour to the floor and melt it carefully over the hole using a lighter, match or blowtorch, taking care not to blacken the wax by getting the flame too close. Allow the melted wax to drip into the hole and, when hardened, use a sharp blade to scrape off any that is proud of the floor.

Removing adhesive hooks

Sometimes when you try to remove a self-adhesive hook from a door it will take paint and maybe the surface of the wood with it! This can be avoided by first warming the hook with a hairdryer, which will loosen the glue and enable the hook to be prised off with a blunt knife. Any glue that remains on the door can be removed using white spirit.

Soften your paintbrushes

If you find that the bristles of many of your paintbrushes have become a bit hard they can easily be softened by soaking them in hot, freshly boiled vinegar. When they have been restored to soft, useable brushes again wash well in soapy water before use.

Metal lubrication

Put a drop of turpentine or vinegar onto the drill bit when drilling into hard metal; it will act as an effective lubricant and make the job a smoother task.

Reusable brush cleaner

After you have used brush cleaning fluid or turpentine don't be too quick to throw the dirty liquid away. If you allow the sediment to settle to the bottom of the jar overnight and then decant the clear liquid above you can reuse it the next time you need to clean paintbrushes.

Tiny paint jobs

For coping with very small paint jobs such as touching up marks and scratches, make a suitable tiny paint applicator by bending a pipe cleaner into a triangle.

Paint tin lids

When you have finished using a tin of paint, smear a little Vaseline (petroleum jelly) around the lip of the lid before replacing. This will make it much easier to remove the next time you come to use it.

Varnish on skin

Use nail varnish remover to effectively remove wood varnish from your hands without leaving your skin smelly or dry.

Grouting tiles

When applying grout between tiles, cotton wool buds are very useful. Excess cement is gathered up by the soft heads and they leave smooth lines. They will also reach into those awkward corners where your fingers or other grouting tools may fail.

Emergency filler

If you have some small cracks or holes to fill before painting and you don't have any filler then use toothpaste. Allow to dry, smooth off gently with sandpaper and paint as normal. No one will ever know!

Homemade cutting in brush

To paint awkward corners of a window frame or edges of a wall or ceiling requires a small brush with tapering bristles. These are called 'cutting-in' brushes and are available from the DIY store – some with angled bristles. If you have not got one then you can make your own quick version by simply fixing an elastic band tightly around the top of the bristles of an ordinary paintbrush (the smallest you have). This will bind the bristles closely together and allow you to paint those difficult places.

Spraying parts of a bicycle

If you are painting something awkwardly shaped, like a bicycle, and you don't want to paint all of it, protect with clingfilm the areas that you don't want to cover and use a paint sprayer – it's much quicker. Do this outside, on a still day, with protection for the surface you are working on and for your breathing.

Curling corners

If you find that you suffer the occasional curling of the corners of wallpaper but don't want to mix up a load of paste for the small job of re-sticking them, there is a quick and easy solution. Simply paint the back of the offending corner with egg-white and leave until tacky before pressing down firmly.

Paint-free arms

If you have ever had paint drip down the handle of your brush onto your wrist and arm when you are panting above your head you will know how annoying this can be! It is a good idea to make a slit in the middle of an old bath sponge and push the paintbrush handle through this before you start work. Any drips of paint will be caught and adsorbed by the sponge instead of running down your arm or dropping onto your hands and face. Alternatively, if you wear a rubber glove and turn the cuff up, this will collect any paint drips. Remember to remove the glove carefully when you have finished.

Protect soft metal

Drilling through soft metal can cause rough edges to the hole or a bend in the metal at the point where the drill enters. This can easily be avoided by sandwiching the metal between two pieces of wood and drilling though the three pieces at once.

Emergency paste

After you have finished a wallpapering job don't throw away all of the paste. Save a little in a screw top jar just in case you need to re-stick a stray piece of paper later.

Wiring a plug

When you look at the inside of a UK plug the contact at the top is always used for the earth wire, if required. But what about the other two connections? Which is for live and which is for neutral? Well, a good way of remembering is that the neutral or bLue wire goes to the left connection (L for left) whilst the live or bRown wire goes to the right connection (R for right).

Clear drains

Lingering waste that might block up an outside kitchen drain can be shifted with the boiling water used to cook potatoes. If you get into the habit of disposing of your potato water in this way then your drains will always run clear.

Don't leave brushes

Try to clean and dry paintbrushes as soon as you have finished using them. It is much easier to remove wet paint from a brush than dried paint. Also don't leave brushes standing in water as this will swell the wood and there will be an increased chance of the bristles falling out.

Starting to wallpaper

Always read the back of the wallpaper sleeve and follow the instructions to the letter. Even if you have hung wallpaper before, the particular paper you are hanging may need slightly different treatment. Always start hanging the paper by working away from the light source. This way you stand less chance of seeing the seams of the paper when it has dried. Remember that wallpaper paste is a powder mixed with water, so, when wallpapering around electric switches and electric sockets always turn off the power at the mains fuse box.

Common types of wallpaper

- **Pulps.** The cheapest type of wallpapers being just paper with a printed pattern. Easy to hang (and strip off!).
- **Woodchip.** Relatively cheap wallpaper with small chips of wood on the finished side. Ideal for hiding minor defects in walls.
- **Washable.** More resistant to stains and marks and can be regularly wiped down.
- **Vinyls.** The vinyl skin makes these papers largely impervious to water. Washable, tough and ideal for kitchens and bathrooms.
- **Anaglyptas.** Plain embossed patterned papers which are normally painted over.
- **Embossed.** These are embossed patterned wallpapers with a decorative finish.
- **Blown vinyl.** These are like the embossed wallpapers except with a vinyl to give a tougher surface.
- **Flocks.** These have raised patterns in fibres which look and feel like velvet. Easily marked as the natural tendency is to reach out and touch!
- **Hand-printed.** Very expensive. Usually supplied untrimmed and should only be hung by professional decorators.

Overhead power

If you are rearranging a workshop or garage and thinking about installing more power sockets, then consider putting some in the ceiling positioned over the area where you will be using power tools. These sockets can be more accessible than wall mounted ones and will eliminate tripping over trailing cables.

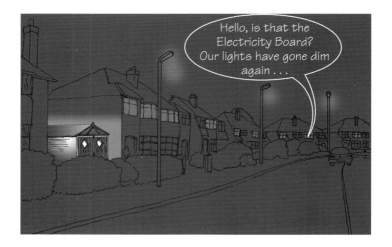

Measuring wallpaper

Make life easier when measuring lengths of wallpaper by using Blu-Tak to hold the top of the paper to the wall. This leaves both hands free to mark the correct length at the bottom.

White-only paintbrushes

No matter how mush you clean a brush after using coloured paint, there will still be a residue of paint left which can slightly discolour white paint. It is always best to keep a couple of brushes of different sizes specifically for white paint only.

Cutting plywood

When sawing plywood, prevent it from splitting by sticking a piece of masking tape over the area to be cut. The tape can be marked with a cutting line using a pencil or fine marker pen.

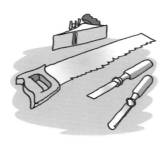

Sealing paper joints

After you have finished wallpapering bathrooms or kitchens use a thin line of clear varnish to seal the paper joints which can peel in these often steamy environments.

Sticking drawers

Rubbing the end of an old candle along sticking drawer runners and the drawer itself will grease and lubricate the moving parts. The drawer should then move effortlessly!

Useful dental floss

If you are working in a confined space where a dropped washer or nut would be almost impossible to retrieve then dental floss could be the answer! Tie one end of a long piece of floss to the washer or nut and the other end to something solid. When the job is complete the dental floss can be easily cut off or, with a nut, it may have already been cut off by the threading action.

Secure hammer handle

To ensure that a new hammer handle is installed securely, before inserting into the hammer head cover the end of the shaft with epoxy resin glue.

Sticking shuttering

If you are laying areas of concrete you may need to make a retaining edge to the areas from pieces of wooden board called shuttering. When the concrete has set the boards are removed and the result is a nice flat edge to the concrete. Sometimes, however, the concrete will stick to the boards making them almost impossible to remove. To avoid this happening, coat the side of the board that will be in contact with the concrete with engine oil before use.

Blocked sink or bath

A blocked sink or bath waste pipe can usually be cleared by probing with a flexible piece of plastic curtain wire. This should quickly loosen and shift the blockage which must then be flushed away using a kettle of boiling water. To ensure that sink and bath waste pipes remain clear, periodically tip down a handful of baking soda followed by a cup of vinegar. This mixture should be left for an hour and then flushed away with copious amounts of boiling water. If all your efforts to unblock the kitchen sink have failed, try crumbling three Alka-Seltzer indigestion tablets into the plug hole and then pouring down a cup of white vinegar. If you wait for a few minutes then follow up with hot water, the sink should be clear.

Free running tape

A steel measuring tape will last much longer if it is always retracting smoothly without rubbing. To keep it in this good condition, apply a small spot of car wax onto the tape and wipe it along the length of the tape with a clean cloth. This will protect the tape surface and keep it running smoothly. Remember to repeat this tip after prolonged use of the tape especially if it is being used in a dusty environment.

Change brushes often

If you have a long painting job to undertake make sure that you change your brush every couple of hours. Using the same brush all day will eventually cause it to harden due to collected paint deep in the bristles and cleaning it will become very difficult.

Patching wallpaper

If you need to apply a patch to wallpaper, you can make the repair less noticeable by tearing the edges rather than cutting them. The joins with the rest of the paper are much less obvious.

Concrete paths

If you lay a concrete path or patio, do not leave the surface smooth as it could become slippery and dangerous when wet. Before the concrete has set completely, pat gently across the whole surface with the thin edge of a piece of timber. This will create grooves in the surface of the concrete and the resulting set surface will be a lot safer.

Vinyl floor tiles

Removing vinyl floor tiles can be made much easier by using aluminium kitchen foil. Place the foil over the tile to be removed then move a hot iron around slowly on top of the foil. The tile will gradually become unstuck and can be lifted away.

New pipes

When adding new pipes to a plumbing system lay horizontal pipes so that they fall away slightly from the main vent pipe, to ensure that any air bubbles can easily escape.

Emergency pipe repair

An emergency repair of a burst pipe can be made using a length of garden hose. Split the hose down its length and wrap it around the damaged pipe. Secure the hose in place with three or more jubilee clips then call a plumber!

Cooler drilling

When drilling into masonry a drill bit can get overheated and cause damage to the bit or the drill itself. Avoid this problem by withdrawing the tip every few seconds and allowing it to cool slightly before continuing. Alternatively, with a small spray bottle, squirt water into the hole periodically during drilling.

Rusted screws

Rusted-in screws, such as those in door hinges, can be loosened by first scraping paint and rust from around them and across the slots and then applying a little release oil. After leaving for half an hour touch the top of each rusted screw with the tip of a hot soldering iron. The heat from the soldering iron should expand the screw and break the rust's hold. The previously applied oil will ensure that the screw should now be easy to remove using a tight-fitting screwdriver.

Locating cables

When running an electrical cable under floorboards try using a mirror and torch to locate the cable under the floor. Before you start feeding cables through walls and under floors make a small hook from a piece of a wire coat hanger and push this into the end of the cable. When you can see the cable but cannot quite reach it, there is a chance that you can locate the hook on the end of the cable using another wire coat hanger and pull the cable through.

Painting guttering

Although manufacturers don't usually recommend painting plastic gutters and downpipes, if you want to match them with other colours of your exterior décor you can paint them with two coats of exterior gloss paint of the appropriate colour. The trick is to brush the coats of paint out further than you would if painting a door.

Smoother filler

When mixing wall filler add a few drops of washing up liquid to the powder and water mix and it will be much smoother and easier to apply.

Screw security

If you have screws that you know you will never have to remove and, for security reasons, you don't want anyone else to be able to either, simply drill out the top of the screw slightly with a high speed steel metal drill.

Ladder painting

When painting up a ladder put the paint tin into a larger container, your paintbrush can then be put into the space around the smaller tin, leaving your hands free.

Removing ceiling paper

When taking paper off a ceiling, first put a bin liner over the back of the step ladder into which the bits of paper can be placed as soon as they are removed. This saves a lot of cleaning up at the end of the day and bits of paper being trodden all over the house!

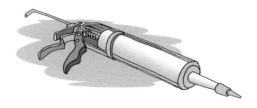

Sharper sewing needles

If you find that your sewing machine needles are becoming blunt, they can be easily sharpened by making a few stitches through a piece of emery cloth!

Handy scraper

If you need a sharp scraper to remove flecks of dried paint from glass, for instance, then you can easily make one using a razor or Stanley knife blade held in the 'jaws' of a large bulldog stationery clip.

Firmer screws

If screws seem to be always working loose then you can ensure a firmer fix by removing the screws and dipping the threaded tips in either PVA glue, nail varnish or oil based paint. This is a particularly good tip to use when putting together flat-packed furniture, where many of the screw holes are pre-drilled. The screws can often work loose, especially if the furniture is moved around.

Homemade rubber mallet

If you need a rubber mallet in a hurry, create a temporary one by making a small hole in a tennis ball and pushing this over the head of an ordinary, metal hammer.

Cutting worktops

Whenever you need to cut a wooden kitchen worktop do so from the top using a jigsaw with a blade that only cuts on the downward stroke not both ways. This will ensure that the top cut edge of the worktop does not become chipped.

Shabby sash cords

When you are renovating or just painting a genuine sash window the white cord can often spoil the final look of the job by appearing shabby and off colour. To avoid having to go to the trouble of replacing the sash cord simply coat it with white canvas shoe dye. This is obtainable with a sponge applicator making it easy to apply to the cord.

Dusty drilling

When drilling into a wall you will inevitably get brick dust falling everywhere and it is not always possible to protect every surface from getting covered, especially in awkward places. There are a few ways to solve the problem. Get an assistant to hold a vacuum cleaner nozzle close to the end of the drill bit as you are drilling. Alternatively tape an open envelope or even a dustpan to the wall just below your drill position to catch the brick dust.

Efficient pasting

When pasting wallpaper always adopt the 'herringbone' effect and move your pasting brush up the centre of the paper then from the centre to sides working from one end of the length of paper to the other. This will ensure an even and more efficient covering of the paste.

Magnetic storage

Every tool box eventually ends up with small screws and nails rattling around. Keep these tidy by sticking them to a small magnet as a temporary measure. When you get around to tidying up your tool box, all these oddments will be together ready for sorting and filing away in the correct places.

Easier hand cleaning

Before beginning any potentially messy DIY job, rub hair conditioner or Vaseline (petroleum jelly) over your hands. Dirt and grime are less likely to stick to your skin. After you have finished your task you should find it is much easier to wash everything off your hands.

Some of the commercially available products for removing paint from skin can cause irritation. Cooking oil, however, will remove most paint from skin without any adverse effects. After the paint has been removed the area should be washed with soap and warm water. Window cleaning liquid is also pretty good at removing paint from your hands.

Homemade level

If you are putting up a shelf and you don't have a spirit level then it is easy to make your own temporary one. Fill a glass two-thirds full with water and stand it on a surface that you know is perfectly level (a kitchen worktop will usually suffice). When the water is dead still in the glass, mark the position of its surface on the glass with a marker pen. Now when you come to put up your shelf you can use the glass of water to ensure it is perfectly level.

Storing paint

When you have finished with a tin of paint and want to
store the remainder make sure the lid is on tight and turn
it upside down for a few seconds before turning it back
upright; this will allow for an airtight seal to form around
the lid so that when you reuse the tin there won't be a
thick skin on top of the paint. If you are sure that the lid is
on tight and there is little chance of the tin of paint being
moved a lot during storage then you can actually keep the
tin in its upside down position.

Make sure that you label any tins of leftover paint with
a line on the outside of the tin which quickly shows you
the level of the paint inside. If you find that you only have
small amounts of paint left then these can still be very
useful for touching up. However, even a little air in a tin
will dry up these small amounts of paint, so transfer them
instead into small, airtight containers and label with the
paint colour and area of use in the house.

63

Spanners

Always use the correct size spanner when undoing nuts. Using an ill-fitting or adjustable spanner can round off the nut making it difficult to use next time. If you don't have the correct size spanner then use one slightly larger and introduce a 'shim' such as a 1p or a 5p piece, between the spanner head and the nut. The shim may need to be tapped into place with a hammer for a really good tight fit.

Interior damp

One chore which should never be put off until another day is treating interior damp. If left it can become a serious hazard and more costly to correct. Here are some exterior causes of interior dampness and simple remedies:

Sagging / broken gutter - replace
Blocked downpipe hopper - clean out regularly
Cracked downpipe - replace
Cracked rendering - renew rendering
Faulty pointing - cleanout and re-point
Porous bricks – give two coats of water repellent brick sealant

Clean drill holes

If you try to insert a raw plug into a freshly drilled hole in masonry, often it will not penetrate far enough due to a blockage of drill dust from the brickwork. Get into the habit of cleaning the dust from the hole first by blowing into it using a bendy type of drinking straw.

Masonry paint preparation

When painting the outside walls of a house using masonry paint, never prepare the walls using a wire brush to rub down as tiny bits of steel wire from the brush may become embedded in the wall. Most masonry paints are water based and of course water and steel will give you rust. This is the cause of the brown lines often seen on exterior paintwork, where the paint has caused rust on nails in the wall or on wire from a wire brush.

Pre-winter tasks

Remember the following and make the winter more manageable:

- Stock up on salt or grit to cope with icy paths and drives.
- Invest in a snow shovel – just in case!
- Make sure that doors and windows are well-fitting and sealed to minimise drafts. Consider hanging longer or thicker curtains to improve insulation.
- Check that all pipes are sufficiently lagged to minimise the risk of freezing.
- Check on loft insulation to see that it is all in place and sufficiently thick to do a good job.
- If you have an open fire then get the chimney swept well in advance of the constant use that it will get over the cold period.
- Have the central heating boiler serviced before it decides to break down just as the big freeze hits town!

Drill bit storage

To avoid any loose drill bits becoming lost or damaged, keep them in an old hard spectacle case to protect them. This also serves as a handy way of carrying the drill bits in your pocket without making holes.

Soldering tips

- To keep the tip of your soldering iron clean during use, regularly rub it over a piece of steel wool stapled to your workbench.

- So that you always have a piece of solder wire handy when you need it, wrap a length around the electrical cable of the soldering iron or clip a piece to the iron with a large bulldog clip.

- When soldering small parts together try using magnets, plasticine or Blu-Tak to hold them in place.

- So that you can see every tiny hole in a metal bucket that needs soldering, shine a light under the container and the places where solder is required will be clearly visible.

Plasterboard

When cutting plasterboard there is no need to blunt your good saw or use a power tool. Simply score one side with a trimming knife, snap along the scored line then carefully turn the sheet over and score and snap along the other side. The result is just like a perfect cut!

When fixing plasterboard to a ceiling and you have no available help, then make up two T-shaped props so they fit just under the plasterboard surface when it is in position. These will be invaluable in keeping the board in place while you fix the screws or nails.

Tool belt

When working on a DIY task that requires a number of different tools then use a tool belt to carry them - either strapped to your waist or, if you are working off the ground, tied around the upper part of the ladder. Tools placed on the top of a stepladder are often out of view and therefore dangerous.

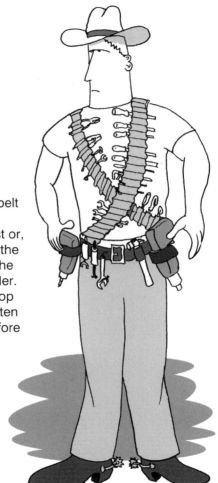

Paint smells

Some people are badly affected by paint odours. Leaving an onion cut in half in the room will remove a vast proportion of the odour or, alternatively, try adding vanilla extract to the paint at a ratio 2 teaspoons to 4 litres. This really works well and does not adversely affect the paint.

Copper pipe repair

A split copper pipe can be temporarily repaired by placing a matchstick or other sliver of wood over the split, covering with melted candle wax and wrapping up with plumber's tape.

Drill depth

Judging just how deep to drill can be difficult once you start drilling. Gauge the depth easily by marking the drill bit at the correct place with a coloured crayon, rubber band or masking tape. When your marker reaches the surface of the wood or masonry you know that the hole is the correct depth.

Bent bristles

If the bristles of your paintbrush are bent because they have been squashed in storage, simply hold them in the steam of a boiling kettle of water for a few minutes then pull them gently back into shape. Take care as the bristles may be hot!

Door tops

Whenever you paint a door or door frame remember to paint the top as well. Even though this area will never be seen it is where dust often accumulates. Removing the dust is much easier if the wood has been painted with gloss paint.

Pasting bucket

When wallpapering, use a plastic mop bucket as a paste container. The pasting brush can be rested in the mop wringing section and any paste drips will fall back into the bucket.

Storing manuals

Instruction manuals for DIY tools and other appliances around the home should always be kept together for easy reference. A small, old suitcase, that can be kept easily accessible, serves as a useful storage place.

Ladder angle

A ladder should always be leaned against a wall or other surface so that the foot of the ladder is one measure out for every four measures in height. So for a 12' ladder its base should be 3' out from the wall. If you are ever uncertain about whether your ladder is positioned correctly always get the help of someone else who can stand at the bottom and hold or 'foot' the ladder for you.

Paint filter

If you have a tin of paint that has acquired a few lumps but you do not want to go to the trouble of decanting the whole tin then there is a simpler option. Cut a piece of fine wire mesh into a circle so it just fits into the top of the paint tin. Let this circular sieve drop slowly through the paint to the bottom of the tin. As it drops through it will push any lumps to the bottom leaving only nice liquid paint above and ready to use.

String dispenser

If you can never find the ball of string when you need it, or when you do it is always knotted up then try this. Get a small plastic funnel and fix it to the wall of the shed or garage so that it stays in an upright position. Place the ball of string in the top of the funnel threading the loose end through the narrow bottom. Whenever you need a length of string it is always to hand and knot free.

Child safety

It seems an obvious statement to make, but keep all DIY tools out of the reach of children. The kids may have watched you do many DIY tasks and decide to have a go themselves. The results could be disastrous – for the kids and your house!

Dripping taps

If you have an irritating dripping tap, don't fancy tackling it yourself and can't get a plumber for a day or so, then tie a piece of string around the end of the tap and dangle this into the plug hole. The dripping water will then flow silently down the string and into the drain. This should give you a bit of peace until the plumber arrives.

Leftover wallpaper

Use leftover pieces of wallpaper to decorate different sized cardboard boxes. These can be used as attractive storage containers on top of wardrobes.

Dripping paint tin

If you find that you are a messy painter and you always seem to get drips of paint down the side of the tin then reduce the risk of getting the paint getting onto any surface by standing the tin on a paper plate.

Rubber-backed carpet

If you are laying rubber-backed carpet or underlay onto a tiled floor, first cover the tiles with newspaper or brown paper. This will prevent the rubber from sticking to the tiles, an advantage should you ever want to change the floor covering.

Cutting marble

Amazingly you will find that marble is not much harder than oak and can be cut by using an ordinary panel saw and re-sharpening often during the cutting.

Homemade tile glue

This may seem like an odd tip but it really works! If a wall tile falls off and you have no tile glue in the house, you can make your own using some jam. Heat the preserve to boiling point and apply to the back of the fallen tile using a paintbrush. Push the tile into place and hold it for a few minutes and you will find it will stick fast. Grout as normal and no-one will ever know!

Sinking ladder

When using a ladder on soil outside, there is always a chance that it could slip or sink into the ground. Standing the ladder on a board will help to avoid this happening. To be really sure of no slipping, nail a piece of wood across the board and place the ladder on the board so that the piece of wood wedges against it and stops the ladder from slipping backwards away from the wall.

Perfect right-angle

To get an exact 90 degree angle, take three lengths of straight timber – 3 ft, 4 ft and 5ft. Nail or screw these together to make a triangle as shown below ensuring that the finished side lengths are exactly as shown. As long as your measuring is accurate, this will result in a true 90° corner. The other two angles will be 30° and 45°. You will then have a useful and decent sized right angle for many uses around the house and garden.

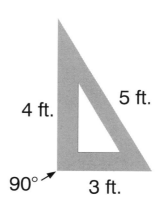

Wood drilling

* Always use a proper wood drill bit for drilling into timber. Masonry or metal drilling bits will often heat up and scorch the wood. The smell might be pleasant but the look of the wood surface may be marred.

* If using a large wood drill bit to drill a deep hole into timber then withdraw it occasionally to keep the hole free and prevent the bit getting jammed with wood dust.

* Always drill pilot holes in wood before trying to fix screws in order to stop the wood from splitting.

Loose leg

A loose wooden chair leg can be secured by removing
it from the base of the chair and wrapping the loose end
with a small strip of nylon, elasticated stocking. Then
apply strong epoxy wood glue to both the stockinged end
and the hole in the base of the chair before re-inserting.

Long timber cuts

When sawing down a long length of timber, cut small wedges out of scrap timber and insert these periodically into the cut as you progress. This will help to stop the saw blade from jamming.

Leaky watering can

If you do not possess a soldering iron, a small hole in a galvanised watering can is easily repaired by sealing it with enamel paint.

Power tool protection

When using power tools inside or outside, always use a plug-in Residual Current Device (RCD). This will protect you from electrocution should you damage the cable on the power tool or should any fault occur during use.

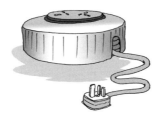

Squeaky hinges

If you have a squeaking door then try using Vaseline (petroleum jelly) to lubricate the hinges. This will work just as well as oil and won't run down the paintwork or drip onto the carpet.

Wallpapering with wood-chip

If you are papering a wall with wood-chip paper and intend to paint over it afterwards then tear the sides of each strip of paper. This way no seams will show through after painting.

Creaking stairs

The irritating noise of creaking stairs can be silenced by using PVA glue. First, with a chisel, prise a small gap between the creaking stair board and the riser. Then, using a piece of cardboard as a spreader, fill the gap with PVA glue.

Tyre pressures

It is always important to keep car tyres at the recommended pressures. Remember that these may differ from front to rear. Under inflated tyres can increase fuel consumption by 10% or more and will weaken the casing as well as wearing the tread on the outside edges. Over inflated tyres will give you less grip than is required by your vehicle. Tyres also deflate as the temperature decreases by approximately one pound of pressure for every 10 degrees Fahrenheit drop in temperature.

Glass protection

To stop any stray paint sticking to the glass when painting window frames, apply a film of petroleum jelly to the vulnerable edge of the glass. When the paint is dry it can easily be rubbed off the protected surface. Alternatively protect the glass from paint by laying strips of dampened newspaper along the edges. This is easily removed when the painting has been completed.

Splitting wood

To prevent wood splitting when hammering in a nail use a very small drill to make a guide hole in the wood. This need only be a very tiny hole to do the trick. If the hole is too large then the nail will not provide the required firm fixing. Alternatively, if you haven't got a small drill then simply blunt the sharp end of the nail first and this will help to prevent splitting.

Loose fixing plug

If the hole that you have drilled for a plastic fixing plug is slightly too wide then don't risk the fixing not being completely secure because of the loose plug. Put some filler in the hole first and push the rawlplug into this so it is flush with the surface, removing any excess filler that oozes out. Let it set before driving home the screw.

Rusty lock

If you find that an old lock has become rusty and keys no longer turn in it, before dismantling the mechanism or buying a new lock, try pouring cola into it through the keyhole. You can do this with a spray gun or a syringe.

Paint roller tray

Avoid spending hours cleaning a paint roller tray simply by covering it with aluminium kitchen foil or cling film before use. This protective covering can be removed and disposed of after use.

Hard putty

If stored putty has hardened, soften it by putting it into a plastic bag and placing it into a bowl of hot water for a time. An occasional squeeze will tell you when it is usable. To avoid this happening always store unused putty by wrapping it completely in aluminium kitchen foil.

Fuse testing

To test a fuse use a torch with the battery cover end removed. Hold the fuse with one end touching the battery and the other touching the torch casing. If the bulb lights when you switch on the torch, then the fuse is OK.

Dust catcher

When drilling overhead you will no doubt get bits of wood shavings or plaster etc… falling over you. Apart form wearing goggles to protect your eyes you can catch all the bits that fall by firstly pushing the drill bit through a paper or plastic cup with the open end pointing upwards.

Cleaning scrapers

Rusty scrapers and filler knives are easily cleaned by rubbing with a metal soap pad. Dip the pad into turpentine and rub vigorously. Avoid using water as this will lead to the tools rusting.

Split tool handles

If you have a wooden handled tool that has the beginnings of a split along its length then an emergency repair can be made using one or two jubilee clips of the correct diameter. If this works and you don't mind the look – it could end up as a permanent repair!

Foam cutting

Foam rubber that needs to be cut into shape for seating can be difficult to cut smoothly. Use an electric carving knife to make the job smoother and quicker, and it does no harm at all to the knife.

Blistering paint

A common problem when painting exterior woodwork is that the paint blisters as it dries. This is caused by moisture becoming trapped under the paint film. This causes the paint to expand as it dries and as it can't move sideways it moves away from the surface causing a blister. The cure is to simply wait until the paint has dried, rub down the blister, make sure the surface to be painted is perfectly dry and start again. A good rule is not to do any painting outside after 3.30pm as the temperature starts to drop and damp in the air will settle on all surfaces.

Floorboard gaps

Gaps between floorboards can be filled by mixing an amount of wallpaper paste to a very stiff consistency and adding shredded brown paper. Fill the gaps with the mixture and leave slightly proud of the floor. When dry, sand, stain and seal to match the other floorboards.

Clear car windows

On a foggy morning a car's windscreen and windows can continually mist over. Avoid this happening by rubbing a cut, raw potato over the exterior of all the glass. When it dries the window will stay mist free. To keep car windows frost free on an icy morning, coat them the previous night with a solution of three parts vinegar to one part water.

Smoother sawing

A wood saw will cut through timber a lot smoother and without snagging if the teeth of the saw are first rubbed with soap.

Fuse replacement

If a fuse blows ALWAYS replace it with one of the same rating. Don't be tempted to use a 13amp fuse to replace a lower rated fuse, even as a temporary measure, because you will probably forget to change it and the appliance will be unsafe. It is also very important to try to find out why the fuse blew in the first place.

For appliances up to 700w the fuse should be 3amp
For appliances between 700w and 1200w the fuse should be 5amp.
For appliances over 1200w the fuse should be 13amp

Nailing tips

- Dip large nails in paraffin or rub them with soap to help them go in smoothly.

- Try to offset a run of nails along a strip of wood, as keeping to the same grain could cause splitting.

- Use a comb or a piece of cardboard with a v-notch to hold a nail in place whilst hammering. This can save on bruised fingers!

- Before driving nails into plaster, heat them first and they will go in more smoothly.

Safer drilling

Whenever you have to drill into walls or ceilings use a battery operated wire/pipe detector to avoid drilling into cables or pipes hidden in the wall. Even if you think you know where these are, don't take the risk – you could easily be mistaken and the results could be costly. Pass the cable/pipe detector over the area of wall or ceiling that you are going to drill into and a visual or audible signal will inform you of the exact position of any hidden services.

Tar on cars

There are a few good ways that you can try to remove tar marks on car paintwork. Rub the marks with margarine, and leave for a few hours before wiping off with a damp, soapy cloth. You can mix bicarbonate of soda with enough water to make a paste and rub this onto the tar mark, which should lift away easily. Finally a few drops of lighter fluid or WD-40 lubricating oil on a soft cloth and rubbed into the tar should also do the trick. After any of the above methods, wax the area.

Light fittings

Due to the heat from an electric light bulb, over a period of time it can become extremely difficult to unscrew the plastic components on light fittings when it becomes necessary to change the shade etc. Running an ordinary pencil point over the threads before initial assembly will make future dismantling effortless. The graphite from the pencil point is a good heat resisting lubricator.

Tiling tips

- When tiling a bathroom always start on the wall where the bath is.

- For a neat finish, place the cut tiles in a corner so the uncut edge of the tile is next to the adjacent wall.

- When cutting a curved line on a tile, make a template out of a piece of cardboard, place it on the tile and mark with a felt tip pen, then cut with a tile saw.

- Tiling over gloss paint is not recommended as the tiles will only be fastened to the gloss paint and not the wall. Rub down the walls with a rough glass paper to cut through the gloss surface and give the tile adhesive something to grip to.

Painting stairs

When painting wooden stair treads remember to paint them alternately. Only when the first set of treads is completely dry should you paint the others. This will ensure that you will still be able to use the stairs (albeit very carefully!) during the decorating period.

Floating floors

Rather than being nailed or glued to a concrete or plywood sub floor, floating floors, such as laminate flooring, float on top of the sub-floor and should be laid on a moisture resistant membrane specially made for the flooring. Floating floors move with changes in humidity in the room where they are installed. Because of this, a small gap is left around the edges, so that such floors will not buckle, crack or squeak.

You can test a newly laid concrete floor for moisture before laying a floating floor by simply taping a piece of plastic sheet to the floor and leaving overnight. If the floor is wet under the plastic when you take it up the next day then it is too wet to lay the floor.

To make your job easier and quicker hire a compound mitre saw for all the cutting or, better still, buy one to assist with all your other DIY projects as well. After you get your packs of flooring home, acclimatise them by stacking them for at least 48 hrs in the room in which they will be laid. Open each pack as you go. Allow at least a 12mm gap all around the wall when laying your floor; this allows for expansion which will in turn stop the floor from lifting or buckling up.

Drilling metal

When drilling into metal always use a slow drill speed and, to avoid any overheating, place putty around the hole and periodically add a few drops of white sprit into the hole for lubrication.

Stripping old paint?

A good rule of thumb is to strip paint only when it is blistered or cracked, otherwise you are making unnecessary work for yourself. If it isn't affected like this then it only needs rubbing down and re-painting.

Extending cables

If you accidentally cut cables short when fixing a socket or switch and they won't reach the terminals don't panic. Use a strip of plastic block connectors and extend with lengths of the correct size cables, making sure there is enough room for the connectors.

Damp starting

Damp air on a cold winter morning can give you real trouble in starting the car. If this happens then use a hairdryer to dry out the engine, especially any electrical contacts.

Brass screws

When screwing brass screws into hardwood first coat the screw with soap or candle wax. This will lubricate the screw and stop the screw head from snapping off. You could also drill a very fine pilot hole into the wood first, making inserting the screw easier and safer.

Stronger joints

When gluing a wooden joint sprinkle a few strands of fine steel wool on one of the glued surfaces before joining; this will produce a much stronger bond.

Sink blockages

When you are clearing a blockage in a sink, basin or bath with a plunger then use a damp cloth to cover the overflow before you begin plunging. This will increase the pressure and your efforts will be more effective.

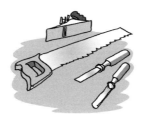

Patience when papering

When pasting wallpaper, be a bit patient and leave the pasted paper to expand and contract for a few minutes before hanging (it should tell you how long on the wallpaper sleeve). This will stop the wallpaper joints opening and/or riding up when the paper has been hung.

Doorstop

An old wooden cotton reel can be nailed to the floor to act as a doorstop. You can blend it in by painting it to match the colour of the floor covering.

Summer heating check

It may not be something that you would immediately think of but always run you central heating system at least once during the summer time, as this will help to keep the pump impeller free and avoid winter problems.

Cutting pipes

To cut a pipe perfectly square without having to mark around the pipe with a pen, simply place a piece of paper around the pipe so that the edges are lined up and use this as a guide for the hacksaw.

Matching filler

If you have cracks to fill in a wall before painting, mix a little of the paint with the filler you intend to use on the walls. When the filler dries it will be the same colour as the walls will be and the repairs will be invisible after one coat of paint.

Lop-sided pictures

Avoid the irritation of slipping pictures by wrapping a piece of adhesive tape around the centre of the string or wire on the back of the pictures before hanging.

Filling cracks

If you have mixed your own decorating filler to fill cracks then it can be applied more effectively using an old icing bag rather than trying to force the filler into areas using a pallet knife.

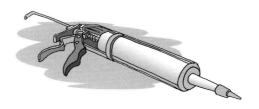

Clean taps

Before you start applying emulsion to the walls or ceiling in the bathroom wrap the taps, shower head etc. in cling film to keep them safe from drips of paint and your inevitable messy hands.

Mini paint applicator

A useful way of coping with those fiddly paint jobs is to recycle a used shoe polish container. Wash out the sponge and the container and fill with emulsion.

Quick plumb line

If you need a plumb line in a hurry and you do not have a proper, shop bought one, then you can easily make one by simply hanging a bunch of keys from a piece of string.

Painting lead

When painting lead first rub the metal with the cut face of half a raw potato. The paint will then stay on the lead even though the lead expands and contracts.

Broken bulbs

Sometimes, when you come to remove a light bulb that has blown, the bottom of the bulb becomes broken and is left stuck in the base of the lamp holder. First turn off the power and then carefully push a carrot into the remainder of the broken bulb. Use this as a handle to twist out the broken bulb base, and then discard it safely.

Sponge paint effects

For sponge painting an internal wall you will need:

A bucket of water
Natural sea sponge (synthetic won't do)
Coloured emulsion (the more varieties, the better effect)
A paint tray
Some old newspaper or a roll of old wallpaper turned upside down
A roll of masking tape
A brush

1. If you have old wallpaper turn it pattern side down and tape it down to a flat surface.
2. Pour some emulsion into the tray to a depth of only 5 or 6 mm.
3. Drop the sponge into the bucket of water, remove and squeeze out most of the water.
4. Holding the damp sponge dab it into the emulsion in the tray.
5. At this point don't go dabbing the walls, as you will get big blobs. Instead dab the paper you have stuck down until you start to transfer the texture of the sponge onto the paper.
6. Now dab the wall with the sponge until you need to reload with paint. Repeat the process until you have gone over the area you want with that particular colour.
7. Now drop the sponge into the bucket of water, change the paint colour in the tray and start all over again. Six to eight different colours looks really nice.
8. For an even finish use the same side of the sponge from the beginning to the end of the job.
9. Never allow another person to take over halfway through as their technique will always differ from yours regardless of how much tuition you give them!

Smoothing wallpaper

When you are hanging non-embossed wallpaper, instead of using a brush to smooth the paper onto the wall, try using a clean, dry paint roller.

Suspending paintbrushes

Whenever you need to soak a paintbrush by suspending the bristles in a jar then attach two clothes pegs to the brush handle. These will rest on the lip of the jar and prevent the bristles from coming into contact with the bottom of the jar and becoming bent.

Broken tiles

To remove a broken tile, first stick two pieces of masking tape across the tile, from corner to corner, to make an 'X'. Then, with a 5mm masonry bit, drill holes through the tape at small intervals but no deeper than the tile thickness. Next, using a small chisel, carefully remove the grout from around the broken tile. Finally, using a cold chisel and hammer, chip at the tile from the pre-drilled centre 'X' and the pieces should easily come away.

Frozen pipes

If you find that water pipes have frozen, don't be tempted to use a blowtorch to thaw them as this can easily cause the pipes to split. Instead use hot water bottles wrapped around the frozen area of pipe or blow warm air across the pipes with a hair dryer.

Outside door

Whenever you paint an outside door be sure to take the door off and paint or varnish the bottom edge. This does add time to the job but if you don't do this then rainwater will run down the door, seep into the bottom through the bare wood and cause it to rot.

Ceiling tiles

When putting up polystyrene ceiling tiles there is always a danger of getting finger marks (or even holes!) in them when trying to press them into place. If you use a soft paint roller you can apply even pressure and the problems are avoided.

Horizontal drilling

A useful way of ensuring that your electric drill is perfectly horizontal before drilling into a wall is to place a loose fitting washer over the drill bit. If the washer stays in the middle of the bit then you are drilling straight. If it falls towards the drill or the wall then you are off line!

Bleeding radiators

When bleeding radiators use a cloth wrapped around
the venting hole as you slowly turn the key to release the
trapped air. This will avoid leaving a dirty water stain on
the wall if the water suddenly reaches the hole and spurts
out. Never remove the valve plug completely as there is
little chance of you reinserting it before the water squirts
out!

Easier washers

When fitting new tap washers and 'O' sealing rings, first
apply petroleum jelly, such as Vaseline, to the washer.
This will make the fitting a lot easier and performance
of the tap a lot better. Don't use oil, however, as this will
attack and deteriorate the rubber.

Cellar steps

If you have cellar steps to paint add a little sand to the paint before use; you will give the painted treads a rough feel and hence a much better grip. As most cellar stairs are pretty steep, it is a good safety tip.

Cleaning a paste brush

Always rinse a wallpaper pasting brush in salted water before washing it properly. This will remove the paste more easily and will help to leave the brush soft and springy.

Fake ebony

If you need a small piece of ebony to make a repair and can't get hold of any then don't despair. You can cheat by obtaining an equivalently sized piece of beech or deal and standing this in a strong solution of ordinary black tea for about three weeks. The result is a piece of fake ebony!

Homemade wood filler

A mixture of sawdust and wood glue makes great homemade wood filler for small holes if you find that you have no proprietary wood filler to hand. The wood shavings used for pet bedding is perfect!

Bolt cutting

If you need to cut a threaded bar or bolt then remember to put the nut on first and screw it on past the place you are going to cut. When you have made the cut take off the nut and it will remove any burred metal with it. If try to get the nut on after cutting then you may have difficulty.

Painting pipes

If you have to paint pipes which are fixed to a wall, cut out a piece of cardboard, place this behind the pipes to be painted and then paint them in the usual way. This will prevent any paint getting onto the wall behind.

Bath sealant

Baths always move slightly when they are filled with water. With this fact in mind always fill a bath with water before sealing around the edge with silicone sealant. This prevents the bath breaking away from the sealant due to the extra weight of the water.

Adhesive hands

After applying any sort of DIY adhesive there is always a chance that some will end up on your hands. This can be removed by dipping your sticky hands into flour. The adhesive will then be much easier to remove and should just peel off.

Painting exterior woodwork

Painting outside surfaces can seem like a daunting job but in reality it is not that bad. Here are some useful tips…

- Badly cracked, flaking, blistering paint must be stripped off. The easiest way is to use a hot air stripper and a stripping knife.

- For safety, drop the hot, stripped paint into a bucket of water.

- Never use a blow torch or hot air gun near windows, especially those with metal frames, as there is a risk of cracking the glass. Instead use a chemical paint stripper after carefully reading the instructions on the tin or bottle.

- Rebates around the windows can be stripped using paint stripper and a special shave-hook.

- Never paint over cracked or loose putty. If it is in poor condition then hack it out with an old table knife and renew.

- After stripping off the paint from outside woodwork, repair any cracks using fillers then rub down with fine glass paper. It is now ready to undercoat and gloss or stain.

Stuck nut

If you have a nut that seems impossible to get off, use a
blow lamp (if it is safe to do so) to heat the nut for a few
seconds. This will expand the metal slightly and, if you are
ready with the correct spanner and a hammer, a sharp tap
should release the nut.

Plumb line shadow

If you are using a plumb line to get that perfect vertical,
maybe for wallpapering, then to avoid marking the wall
with a pencil simply shine a bright light on the line and it
will cast a perfect shadow. You can then use the shadow
line to work to.

Leaky overflow

If you have a leaky cistern overflow and can't get it fixed
immediately temporarily stop the leak by tying a wooden
spoon to the ballcock arm and place it across the sides of
your cistern.

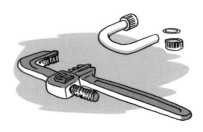

Rubbing door

If you find that a door is rubbing a little on the carpet then there is probably no need to remove the door and plane the bottom. Place a surform blade or 60 grit sandpaper, rough surface uppermost, under the door where it appears to be rubbing and move door quickly backwards and forwards. This should remove just enough of the offending wood to allow the door to swing freely.

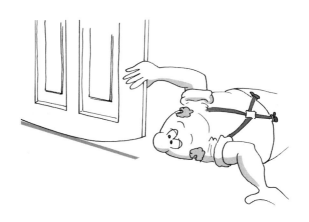

Sawing softwood

When sawing softwoods, instead of drawing a line with a pencil or pen, score the wood with a sharp blade such as a craft or Stanley knife. This will cut the fibres in the wood and makes it easier to start the saw and keep to the exact cutting line.

Gluing

When gluing two surfaces together remember the golden rule - "The thinner the glue line the stronger the joint". Achieve this by gently rubbing the two glued surfaces together until they barely move before clamping together.

Plaster seal

When painting new plaster or any similar porous surface first paint on a solution of water mixed with PVA glue. This will seal the surface and stop the paint from soaking into the plaster, thereby making it go a lot further and giving a much better finish.

Ladder safety

One of the golden rules of ladder work is never to wear slippery soled shoes. Even if you think that the rungs of the ladder have treads that are rough enough to give you a firm footing, don't take chances. One drop of spilled paint or estranged sealant under your feet could be your downfall – literally!

Painting railings

An easy and quick way to paint railings etc. is to use a cheap car cleaning mitten! Dip your 'mittened' hand into the paint, take off any surplus, then grip the railing with the mitten and run your hand up and down. This is much less tedious than using a brush.

Mini-rollers

A variety of neat little paint rollers can be made for painting pipes and other fiddly jobs by using a selection of ladies' foam hair rollers. Ask permission first!

Cable hole

If you have to drill a hole in wood to pass through an electrical cable always ensure that you drill in the direction the cable is going to run. The cable will then run smoothly through the hole without getting snagged. If you need to pass a cable through a tight space then rub the length with car wax first and it should slip through easily.

Bubbly wallpaper

Even the most experienced decorator can suffer the agony of air bubbles in newly hung wallpaper. Remove these easily by cutting into each bubble with a sharp blade and inserting some paste into the hole using a syringe, then flatten gently to the wall using a wallpapering brush.

Removing linoleum

If you are trying to remove linoleum and you find that it is stuck fast with glue, then you can make the job easier by using a warm iron and a tea towel. Place the tea towel over the area of linoleum to be lifted and apply the iron over this just for a few seconds. This should melt the glue and enable you to easily pull up the whole piece of linoleum rather than just fragments!

Magnetic cleaning

When drilling a hole into iron or steel you will often find that fine bits of metal can fall in and are difficult to remove. They can, however, be easily be removed using magnetism! Simply find a steel or iron rod that will fit into the hole, right to the bottom. Press a strong magnet to the upper end of the rod and, keeping it there, remove the rod. The bits of waste metal will be stuck to the end and can be brushed off.

Thinning gloss paint

When using gloss paint it starts to go thick after a while and becomes more difficult to paint with. If this happens all you need do is add a generous squirt of washing up liquid to the paint and give it a good stir. It will then go further, spread better and will not leave brush marks.

Egg

Mushrooms

Bacon

Sausages

Leaking radiator

If you have a leaking car radiator try one of these short
term remedies until you can get to a garage for a repair. If
you can see the leak, then place a piece of chewing gum
over the hole; the heat of the radiator will keep the gum
tacky and should seal the hole. Alternatively try cracking
an egg into the boiling radiator, which should seal the hole
from the inside. Be very careful, however, when opening a
car radiator cap. Cover with a thick cloth first and open it
very slowly to allow the pressurised steam to escape.

Difficult plug

If an electric plug becomes difficult to insert or remove from the socket then try rubbing the metal contacts of the plug with a soft, graphite pencil. Graphite is a natural lubricant and you should find that the plug will slide effortlessly in and out of the socket!

Drilling glass

If you have to drill through a mirror or sheet glass then this procedure will ensure success. First mark the spot for drilling with a felt-tipped pen. Next make a small well of glazing putty and place this over the marked spot so it sticks to the surface but you can still just see the mark. Then fill the well with light oil such as sewing machine oil. Start drilling slowly using a carbide-tipped drill bit. The oil will keep the drill bit cool and prevent the glass from cracking.

Wardrobe doors

When the catches on a wardrobe's doors become worn the doors may be prone to swinging open. A drawing pin, pushed into the top of the bottom edge of the offending door or doors will often prove a cost effective solution to the problem!

Coloured filler

If using filler on stained wood or dark hardwood then add a little instant coffee powder to the filler to make the colour a better match. Experiment with different amounts in a small quantity of filler until you achieve a good colour match.

Oil spillages

Immediately an oil spills occurs, in the garage or on the drive, it should be covered with fresh, dry cat litter. This will quickly and easily soak up the oil. When the oil has been absorbed the litter can be carefully swept up and disposed of. More can then be applied if required. Pouring cola over dried oil or grease stains on a brick driveway can usually effect their removal. If the cola is applied in the evening and left overnight, when it is washed off in the morning the stain should have disappeared.

Cleaning guttering

Guttering should be checked and cleaned on a regular basis both that on the house and also on the garage, garden shed or greenhouse. You should be extra vigilant during the autumn when falling leaves can soon block guttering and down pipes and cause major problems. Even if you have no deciduous trees in your own garden you are not safe. There is a little matter of the wind!

Before cleaning gutters place a bowl or bucket under the down pipe. This will prevent any debris from blocking the drains. You may have to remove a section of the down pipe to allow you to take this precautionary measure but it is worth the trouble.

Wearing a good, strong pair of gloves first remove any leaves, twigs etc… from the gutter troughs. A piece of wood the same shape as the curve of the gutter but slightly smaller can be cut and used as a scraper for a thorough job. Then brush the gutters with a stiff brush and hose the remaining debris down into your waiting bowl of bucket.

Glue pen

A neat little glue brush for fine or inaccessible gluing jobs can be made using the plastic casing of a ballpoint pen and a piece of string. After removing the ink refill from the pen thread the string through the pen's plastic casing. Finally tease out the ends of the string to make the glue brush bristles.

Fencing tips

A few things to consider when erecting wooden garden fencing:

- Check the condition of garden fences regularly and make any repairs immediately. If you wait, a windy night could make the job twice as big, more costly and damage to other property may have occurred.

- Never try to carry out any lasting repairs or erect new fencing in bad weather. By all means take emergency action to temporarily fix the problem but wait until a calm dry day to do it properly.

- Most fencing jobs will require two people. Trying to be a hero on your own could be foolish and lead to injury or, worst still, an inadequate job!

- Always use pressure-treated (also known as 'tanalised') wooden posts as these should carry a guarantee against rot and will last for 10 to 15 years.

- Take the time to run a straight string line to mark the position of the fence run and use a spirit level to check that the posts are vertical and the panels are horizontal.

- Wooden posts can be anchored in place in two ways. You can use either long metal spikes which are driven into the ground and have a square socket at the top to accept the post or by concreting the bottom 18" (450mm) of the post into the ground. If the soil is loose then always use the concrete option but wait at least a day for the concrete to set before fitting the panels.

- Never allow wooden fencing panels to be in contact with the soil as they will eventually rot. If you cannot leave a gap beneath then attach a 6" (150mm) or 12" (300mm) wide, pressure-treated (tanalised) gravel board to the bottom of each panel and let this sit on the soil.

Woodworm treatment

If you discover that you have woodworm in floors then these should be treated both on top and underneath the floorboards for effective control. Remove a few boards and, wearing a protective face mask and goggles, use a garden type pump–up sprayer with a curved lance to spray the affected timber.

Patio laying tips

Here are a few useful things to remember when laying slab path or patio:

- When ordering your slabs allow an extra 15% to 20% for breakages or cutting. You can usually strike a deal with the builder's merchant to return any slabs that are unused.

- Make sure that the surface on which you are laying the slabs is solid. If in any doubt then hire a petrol-driven compactor plate to ensure you have a firm foundation on which to lay. If the ground has been recently dug, the house is under 12 months old or you are in any way unsure about the solidity of the ground then dig out 4" (100mm) depth of soil from the area and compact down a mixture of hardcore and sand to the required level.

- Decide whether you are going to lay the slabs on a dry mix of 6:1 building sand to cement or a wet mortar mix of the same ratio. A dry mix is acceptable for areas that will receive light use and is easy to work with. A wet mix, although a bit trickier to use, gives a far stronger foundation and should be used if you are in any doubt or for areas of heavy usage.

- If you are laying slabs for vehicle use then you should always lay a 6" (150mm) compacted hardcore foundation layer first and use a wet mortar mix as a bed for the slabs. Make sure the slabs that you choose are recommended for vehicles.

- Whether mixing by hand or using a cement mixer, ensure that the sand and cement are thoroughly mixed otherwise the resulting foundation will not be of uniform strength.

- When making a wet mortar mix, the addition of a small amount of washing-up liquid to the water can help to make the mix smoother and easier to use.

- Only make up enough mix – wet or dry – that you can comfortably use in an hour as the mix will start to 'go off' and will not bond successfully to the slabs.

- Always lay slabs on a full bed of mortar mix. Using a 'five blobs of mortar' technique is false economy as there will always be gaps beneath the slabs. If something heavy is dropped on them there is more chance of them cracking.

- When laying slabs always ensure that there is a slight slope away from the house for the run off (or 'fall') for water to drain away. This needs only to be about 1:50 for smooth faced slabs and 1:40 for more uneven-surfaced or 'rivened' slabs.

- Take your time in laying the slabs and check often with a spirit level that you have the required fall. When first offering the slabs onto the mortar mix they should only require only a few taps with a rubber hammer to get them to the correct level. If they look as though they are too proud then lift them and remove some of the mix. Don't be tempted to continue hitting the slab as it will probably break!

- Remember to always leave joints of about 3/8" (10mm) between the slabs. This will allow slabs to be easily lifted should any need replacing. It will also enable you to cope with any slight discrepancies in the sizes of, apparently, similar sized slabs!

- The level of the patio at the house wall must be at least 6" (150mm) below the damp proof course. This is usually visible as an extra wide line of mortar in the brickwork or, in older houses, you may be able to see the edge of pieces of slate that were used. If your patio is built higher than this, the walls will get damp.

- If possible always leave a 2" (50mm) minimum gap between the edge of the patio and the house wall and fill this with gravel. This will ensure that even in the fiercest of storms water will drain away through the gravel.

- For filling in the joints between the slabs you have three choices. You can make up a dry 3:1 mix of building sand and cement and brush this over the surface of the slabs so it fills the joints. The surfaces of the slabs must be perfectly dry to do this as the mix will stick to and this stain damp slabs. Alternatively you could point up the joints using a 3:1 wet mortar mix of building sand and cement. This takes more care but sets quicker and gives a stronger bonding of the slab edges. The final way is to use one of the new air-activated resin jointing compounds such as Geofix. This gives a perfect, hard joint without the difficulties of using wet mortar. It also comes in either grey or buff colours.

And finally...

Probably the best bit of DIY advice you could ever receive is 'measure twice – cut once!' Even if you are sure that the measurement that you have just taken is correct, take it again – just to be sure. Once you have set the drill or saw in motion there is no going back!

Wood types:

Hardwoods

These include Ash, Beech, Cherry, Chestnut, Elm, Lime, Mahogany, Oak (English, imported and Japanese), Rosewood, Teak and Walnut.

Hardwoods are strong and more expensive than softwoods because of their durability and longevity. They are ideal for making good quality furniture and flooring. The wood is seasoned to strengthen it and should have been covered during storage.

Softwoods

These include Cedar, Deal, Hemlock, Larch, Pine, Spruce, Redwood, Whitewood and Yew.

Softwoods may be cheaper than hardwoods but they will not last as long, especially outside. For exterior use they require regular treatment with paints or preservatives to protect the wood from the weather – rain and sun. Softwood can easily become split or warped in storage so check carefully before you purchase.

Sawn or planed?

Sawn timber appears rough as it comes directly from being cut into sections. It is cheaper than planed timber and can be used where its rough appearance cannot be seen, such as in a loft space for rafters and joists.

Planed timber has been machine cut and planed to give a smooth edge. It is slightly more expensive than rough-cut timber but can usually be painted or stained immediately without further sanding.

Block-board

This is made by the high pressure bonding of glued rectangular strips of softwood sandwiched between a veneer of wood such as birch. If the block-board has a single veneer on each side it is called 3-ply or, if it has a double veneer to each face, 5-ply. As the glues used to make block-board are not waterproof it should only be used inside. Painting should be done to each side to retain the tension and shape of the board.

Chipboard

This is made from particles of softwood coated in resin, spread over a flat plate and heat-bonded under high pressure. There are various grades of chipboard – flooring, melamine veneered (Formica), plastic veneered and wood veneered.

Hardboard

This is made by forcing softwood pulp into sheets which, for the standard hardboard sheet, are smooth finished on one side and textured on the other. There are other types of hardboard available – duo faced, medium, oil-tempered, painted, plastic faced and perforated (pegboard).

MDF

MDF stands for Medium Density Fibreboard and is an extremely versatile timber product suitable for a wide variety of interior DIY projects. It cannot be used outside or allowed to get wet. It is made by bonding wooden fibres together under high pressure in a way that gives a very fine texture throughout the timber. As the fibres used are extremely fine it is important to use a face mask when cutting MDF to avoid inhaling the dust particles.

Plywood

This is made by bonding veneers together, face-to-face, with the grains running in alternate directions. Sheets are always bonded either side of a central sheet to keep the tensioning equal. Therefore the thinnest plywood will be made from three sheets of veneer and is known as 3-ply. Thicker and hence stronger plywood is made by adding sheets equally to both sides of 3-ply to make 5-ply, 7-ply etc... There is a more expensive, waterproof type of plywood available for external use.

Remember...

- All of the wood sheets and boards listed above can be bought in a variety of thicknesses. To avoid twisting or warping they should always be stored flat with protection for the sides and corners.

- Long strips of wood or battens are prone to warping whilst in storage so take the time to check these carefully when buying.

- When you give your timber measurements to the timber yard they will assume that they are the sawn timber sizes. If you then ask for planed timber, the finished measurements will be smaller.

Screw types

Single-slot countersunk head screws

These are traditional screws with a long shank and single slot for use with a flat-head screw driver. They are used for general joining work and hinges. 'Countersunk' means that the screw head is shaped so that it can be driven in flush with the surface of the wood etc.

Cross-head, countersunk screws

These are probably the most popular types of screw. These have a cross-shaped slot for the corresponding cross-head screwdriver. This prevents the screwdriver slipping. Philips screws have a slightly different shaped cross-head which lends itself more to driving with a powered screwdriver.

Round-head screws

When these screws are driven in the domed screw head rests on the top of the surface and are easier to remove later if required. They are used to fasten metal to wood, metal to metal or other material. Round-head screws are completely threaded from point to head and the threads are sharp.

Mirror screws

These are most commonly used for fixing mirrors and come in two parts. First there is a countersunk, slotted-head screw which is fixed first. A dome-shaped, chrome cover is then fitted into the top of then screw for a decorative finish.

Chipboard screws

These are similar to the traditional countersunk type of screw but they have a deeper thread to give a better grip into chipboard.

Twin-thread screws

These screws have two deep threads interwoven with each other. This feature, coupled with a narrower shank, give the screws a much better grip.

Self-tapping screws

These are used in tougher materials such as metal and fibreglass. To use self-tapping screws, a pilot hole that is the same gauge of the shank of the screw must first be drilled into the material. As the screw is tightened into the material it cuts a thread.

Clutch-head screws

The heads of these screws have a unique cross pattern which allows the screws to be tightened but not undone. They are used in situations of security such as when fitting locks etc... It is best to use an ordinary screw of the same size first, whilst doing the initial fitting of equipment. This will enable you to make any minor adjustments to the fitting before using the permanent clutch-head screw.

Dry-wall screws

These are thinner than normal screws and have much sharper points. The thin screw heads enable them to be driven easily into the surface of the board or studwork.

Screw measurements

A wood screw is always labelled with two measurements – the screw length and the shank diameter. The length is measured from the tip of the screw to the part of the screw that will eventually be level with the surface of the wood. A gauge number is given to the shank to indicate its diameter i.e 6, 8, 10. The higher the shank number the thicker then screw.

Nail types

Round wire nails

These general purpose nails with a large, round, flat head are mostly used for rough carpentry where appearance is not important but strength is essential. They are inclined to split a piece of wood. Sizes are ¾" to 6" (20mm - 150mm).

Oval wire nails

The heads of these nails can be easily hidden by knocking them below the surface using a nail punch. This makes them most suitable for joinery work where appearance is important. They are less likely to split the wood if driven in with the longer sides parallel to the grain. Sizes are from ½" to 6" (12mm - 150mm).

Round or lost-head nails

These are similar but stronger than oval wire nails. They can easily be punched below the surface of the wood. Sizes are from ½" to 6" (12mm - 150mm).

Galvanised nails

These zinc-coated nails are rust-proof and hence very useful for exterior use.

Hardboard nails

These nails have diamond-shaped heads which are virtually hidden when hammered into hardboard. They are used frequently in carpentry. Sizes are from 3/8" to 1½" (9mm - 38mm).

Masonry nails

These nails are made of hardened steel and are used to fix wood to brick, breeze block and most types of masonry.

Cut floor brads

These are rectangular, with an L-shaped head and are nearly always used for nailing floorboards to joists. Sizes are from 1" to 6" (25mm -150 mm).

Square twisted nails

These comparatively expensive nails offer a more permanent, screw-like grip than plain nails. They have shanks with a spiral twist so they work like screws and twist into the wood.

Annular nails

These nails are useful where very strong joints are required. The sharp ridges round the shanks become embedded in the wood to give a tight grip.

Cut clasp nail

These nails are rectangular in section. Once used they are extremely difficult to remove and hence provide a very strong fixing in wood and pre-drilled masonry. Sizes are from 1" to 6" (25mm -150 mm).

Clout head nails

These are made of galvanized steel, with a large, flat retaining head. This nail is most suitable for soft materials such as plasterboard and roofing felt.

Spring-head roofing nails

These special nails are used for fixing corrugated sheeting to timber. The twisted shank and inverted cup head produces a very strong purchase.

Panel pins

Small, round, lightweight nails used for cabinet-making, fixing small mouldings and other fine carpentry work.

Tacks

Short nails with a wide, flat head, used for fixing carpets to floorboards and for stretching fabric on to wood and other upholstery work.

Sprigs

These are small nail without heads. They are used mainly to hold glass in window frames before applying putty which covers them up. Sizes are from ½" to ¾" (12mm - 19mm).

Upholstery nails

These are available in chrome, brass and other metallic finishes. They are used as secondary fixings with tacks. The dome heads gives a decorative finish when finishing upholstery work such as nailing chair coverings into place. Various head sizes are available.

Staples

These are U-shaped round wire nails with two points to hold lengths of wire in position. Some staples have an insulated lining for fixing flex and electric cable.

Tool lists

Essential tool kit

The basic, essential tool kit for every house should include:

- Screwdrivers – both cross-head and flat blade, or an electric screwdriver with a variety of heads
- Allen keys
- Claw hammer
- Wooden mallet
- Tape measure
- Small adjustable spanner
- Plumber's wrench or large adjustable spanner
- Pliers (with built-in wire cutter / stripper)
- Wood chisel

- Torch (with batteries that work – check regularly!)
- Protective goggles
- Electrical tape
- Plumber's tape
- Small hacksaw
- Selection of nails, screws and plastic fixing plugs
- Selection of different glues – epoxy, wood and PVA
- Spare light bulbs, candles and matches

Wallpapering tools

Pasting table
Pasting brush
Craft knife
Seam roller
Long-bladed scissors
Paperhanging brush
Sponge
Plumb line
Spirit level
Ruler
Pencil
Bucket
Small pair of steps
Blu-Tak

Bricklaying tools

Bricklayer's trowel
Bricklayer's float
Spirit Level
Builder's square
String line
Shovel
Bucket
Hammer and bolster chisel
Measuring tape
Wheelbarrow
Pencil
Builder's spot (board or purpose-made
plastic surface for mixing mortar on)

Tiling tools

Marking pencil
Plumb line
Tape measure
Spirit Level
Tile cutter
Tile nibbler
Tile saw
Tile file
Tile spacers or matches
Adhesive spreader
Grout spreader
Bucket (disposable)
Hammer
Cold chisel
Adhesive
Grout
Sponge
Cleaning cloth

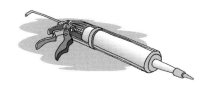

Painting tools

Stiff brush (not wire)
Polyester and lambswool paint rollers and tray
5" emulsion brush
½" paintbrush
1" paintbrush
2" paintbrush
Plumb line
Sponge
Bucket
Ladder
Paint kettles
Wall scrapers
Putty knife
Masking tape
Small screwdriver
Protective sheets
Wood and wall filler
Sealant and application gun
Putty
Various grades of sandpaper and emery cloth

Carpentry tools

Claw hammer
Tape measure
Screwdrivers
Electric drill
Brace drill
Wood drill bits
Utility knife
Wood chisels (½" and ¾")
Mitre box
Rasps and files
Clamps
Sprit level
Crosscut saw
Tenon saw
Plane
Framing square
Carpenter's pencil

Electrical tools

Torch
Pliers
Sharp knife
Wire cutters / stripper
Insulated terminal
    screwdriver
Neon test
    screwdriver
Electrical insulation
    tape

Assorted plastic connector blocks
Assorted fuses
Assorted cable ties
Fuse wire
Spare 3 pin plugs
Spare cable
    1.0mm for lighting circuits
    2.5mm for power circuits and immersion heater
    6.0mm for cooker circuits and showers up to 8.5kw
    10.0mm for cooker circuits and showers over 8.5kw

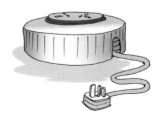

Plumbing tools

Adjustable spanner
Pipe wrench
Water pump (slip-joint) pliers
Plunger
Hacksaw
Blowtorch
Soldering iron,
   solder and flux
Pipe cutter
Knife
Emery cloth
Plumbers tape
   (PTFE or Teflon tape)
Radiator key
Assortment of tap washers
Pipe jointing compound

Wallpaper calculator

When choosing wallpaper always check the batch/shade numbers are the same. Make sure you buy enough wallpaper to finish the job. Any unopened rolls can be returned for a refund.

This chart is for guidance only. For large patterned wallpaper you will need to allow extra rolls for matching.

The distance around the room includes windows and radiators and the wall height is from skirting board.

Distance around room		Number of rolls		
			Height	
(m)	(ft)	2.15m-2.30m 7ft-7.5ft	2.30m-2.45m 7.5ft-8ft	2.45m-2.60m 8ft-8.5ft
9	29.5	4	5	5
10	33	5	5	5
12	39.5	5	6	6
13	42.5	6	6	7
14	46	6	7	7
15	49	7	7	8
16	52.5	7	8	9
17	56	8	8	9
19	62.5	8	9	10
20	65.5	9	9	10
21	69	9	10	11
22	72	10	10	12
24	77	10	11	12
25	82	11	11	13
26	85.5	12	12	14
27	88.5	12	13	14
29	95	13	13	15
30	98.5	13	14	15

Tile calculator

This chart may help you when buying tiles. Remember to buy some extra just in case you suffer breakages.

Tile size		Quantity required	
Metric (mm)	Imperial (in)	per sq. metre	per sq. yard
100x100	4" x 4"	100	84
108x108	4.25" x 4.25"	86	72
150x150	6" x 6"	44	36
200x100	8" x 4"	50	41
200x150	8" x 6"	33	27
200x200	8" x 8"	25	20
225x150	9" x 6"	29	24
225x225	9" x 9"	20	16
250x150	10" x 6"	27	22
250 x150	10" x 10"	16	13
250x250	12" x 8"	17	14
300x200	12" x 12"	11	9
300x300	13" x 13"	9	8

Weight & measure conversions

Length:

1 millimetre (mm)		= 0.0394 inch (in)
1 centimetre (cm)	= 10 mm	= 0.0394 in
1 metre (m)	= 100 cm	= 1.0936 yard (yd)
1 kilometre (km)	= 1,000 m	= 0.6214 mile

1 inch		= 2.54 cm
1 foot (ft)	= 12 in	= 0.3048 m
1 yard	= 3 ft	= 0.9144 m
1 mile	= 1,760 yd	= 1.6093 km

Area:

1 square cm (cm^2)	= 100 mm^2	= 0.1550 in^2
1 square m (m^2)	= 10,000 cm^2	= 1.1960 yd^2
1 square km (km^2)	= 100 hectares	= 0.3861 $mile^2$

1 square in (in^2)		= 6.4516 cm^2
1 square ft (ft^2)	= 144 in^2	= 0.0929 m^2
1 square yd (yd^2)	= 9 ft^2	= 0.8361 m^2
1 acre	= 4,840 yd^2	= 4,046.9 m^2
1 square mile ($mile^2$)	= 640 acres	= 2.590 km^2

Volume:

1 cubic cm (cm³)		= 0.0610 in³
1 cubic decimetre (dm³)	= 1,000 cm³	= 0.0353 ft³
1 cubic m (m³)	= 1,000 dm³	= 1.3080 yd³
1 litre (l)	= 1 dm³	
	= 1000 millilitre (ml)	= 1.76 pint (pt)
	= 2.113 US pt	
1 hectolitre (hl)	= 100 l	= 21.997 gallon (gal)
		= 26.417 US gal

1 cubic in (in³)		= 16.387 cm³
1 cubic ft (ft³)	= 1,728 in³	= 0.0283 m³
1 cubic yd (yd³)	= 27 ft³	= 0.7646 m³
1 fluid ounce (fl oz)		= 28.413 ml
1 pint (pt)	= 20 fl oz	= 0.5683 l
1 gallon (gal)	= 8 pt	= 4.546 l
		= 1.201 US gal

Mass:

1 milligram (mg)		= 0.0154 grain
1 gram (g)	= 1,000 mg	= 0.0353 ounce (oz)
1 metric carat	= 0.2 g	= 3.0865 grains
1 kilogram (kg)	= 1,000 g	= 2.2046 pound (lb)
1 tonne (t)	= 1,000 kg	= 0.9842 ton

1 oz	= 437.5 grains	= 28.35 g
1 lb	= 16 oz	= 0.4536 kg
1 stone	= 14 lb	= 6.3503 kg
1 hundredweight (cwt)	= 112 lb	= 50.802 kg
1 ton	= 20 cwt	= 1.016 t

Temperature conversions

Celsius °C	Fahrenheit °F	Celsius °C	Fahrenheit °F
-30°C	-22°F	16°C	60.8°F
-20°C	-4.0°F	17°C	62.6°F
-10°C	14.0°F	18°C	64.4°F
0°C	32.0°F	19°C	66.2°F
1°C	33.8°F	20°C	68.0°F
2°C	35.6°F	21°C	69.8°F
3°C	37.4°F	22°C	71.6°F
4°C	39.2°F	23°C	73.4°F
5°C	41.0°F	24°C	75.2°F
6°C	42.8°F	25°C	77.0°F
7°C	44.6°F	26°C	78.8°F
8°C	46.4°F	27°C	80.6°F
9°C	48.2°F	28°C	82.4°F
10°C	50.0°F	29°C	84.2°F
11°C	51.8°F	30°C	86.0°F
12°C	53.6°F	40°C	104°F
13°C	55.4°F	50°C	122°F
14°C	57.2°F	60°C	140°F
15°C	59.0°F		

To convert Fahrenheit to Centigrade: $C = 5/9 \times (F-32)$

To convert Centigrade to Fahrenheit: $F = (9/5 \times C) + 32$

Index

Index

Index

Index

Notes

'The Greatest Tips In The World'

'The Greatest Tips In The World' is a unique series of fun and informative hints and tips books, devised and created by Steve Brookes and written by authors who are experts in their field.

This fabulous collection of books will grow each year to cover many home and leisure interests with Gardening Tips, Golfing Tips, DIY Tips, Cookery Tips and Household Tips being the first five titles in the series. With many more to follow, these books will form a most useful compilation for any bookshelf!

For more information about currently available books, forthcoming titles and the authors, please visit:

www.the**greatest**in**the**world**.com**

or write to:

Public Eye Publications
PO Box 3182
Stratford-upon-Avon
Warwickshire CV37 7XW

The Authors

Chris Jones' interest in DIY started at the age of 6 when he took up the parlour parquet flooring with his first tool kit! He qualified as an electrician over 20 years ago and had a successful electrical contracting business for 14yrs. Chris now works as a demonstrator and adviser for a major DIY store. You may have even seen him on TV! Chris is the real 'family man' and is passing on his DIY knowledge and vast experience to his boys Peter & Mark helped by the endless patience of his wife Cathy.

Brian Lee trained as a decorator 35 years ago. After 9 years in the army, Brian developed a passion for crafting useful things out of wood. His job now involves teaching DIY skills (mainly to ladies and children!) with bird tables, nesting boxes and dovecots often being on his project list. Born in Cheshire but now living in Hampshire with his wife Yvonne, Brian is keen on passing on his great DIY know-how to his three grown up children and two grandchildren.